VISION BOARD
CLIP ART BOOK
FOR BLACK GIRLS

Kalishia Winston

YOUR FREE GIFT

As a way of saying thanks for your purchase, I'm offering the eBook *Teach Your Kids to Create Their Future with a Vision Board* for FREE.

To get instant access just go to:

KIDS.KALISHIAWINSTON.COM

Father And Mother I Love You

Friends
MAKE THE
World
Beautiful

LIFE IS
Better With
Friends

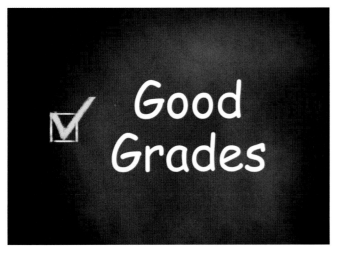

NEW DOG

NEW CAT

NEW PET

I am doing GREAT things for my FUTURE

I have overcome challenges before and will do it again

I never give up on things I really want to achieve

I have what it takes to make all my DREAMS come true

I don't need to be PERFECT to achieve my dreams

I am PROUD of what I've already accomplished

I am in
control
of my
FUTURE

I will not let
others
distract me
from my
GOALS

I
WORK
on my
GOALS
every day

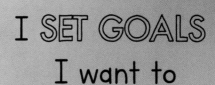

I SET GOALS
I want to
achieve
not those others
want to me set

There is a
time to
push myself
and a time to
rest.

I am
creating new
positive habits
for myself

ask questions	help others	be fair
be kind	be positive	dream big
be grateful	I am enough	I am strong
I am talented	I am brave	I am smart
I want to see	I want to try	I want to learn
things I love	my goals	my plans
I want to achieve	happy	make new friends
never give up	love	hobbies
I will start	I will learn	keep trying
have fun	adventures	be me
be a star	school	every day

Made in the USA
Coppell, TX
28 December 2024

43654263R00024